A+ books

Step-by-Step
Stories

Getting
a Pet,
Step by Step

by J. Angelique Johnson

CAPSTONE PRESS
a capstone imprint

A+ Books are published by Capstone Press,
151 Good Counsel Drive, P.O. Box 669, Mankato, Minnesota 56002.
www.capstonepub.com

Books published by Capstone Press are manufactured with paper
containing at least 10 percent post-consumer waste.

Library of Congress Cataloging-in-Publication Data
Johnson, J. Angelique.
  Getting a pet, step by step / by J. Angelique Johnson.
    p. cm.—(A+ books. Step-by-step stories)
  ISBN 978-1-4296-6024-2 (library binding)
  1. Dog adoption—Juvenile literature. 2. Pets—Juvenile literature. I. Title.

SF426.5.J646 2012
636.7'0887—dc22

2011002615

Credits
Shelly Lyons, editor; Ted Williams, designer; Marcie Spence, media researcher; Sarah Schuette, photo stylist;
    Marcy Morin, studio scheduler; Eric Manske, production specialist

Photo Credits
Alamy Images: Ian Dagnall, 12 (right); Capstone Studio: Karon Dubke, cover, 1, 4, 5, 6, 8, 9, 10-11, 11,
12-13, 14, 15, 16-17, 18, 20, 21, 22, 23, 24, 25, 26, 27, 28, 29; iStockphoto: alexsl, 12 (left), DenGuy, 19
(inset); Shutterstock: aspen rock, 19, EDHAR, 12 (middle), Ivan Montero Martinez, 7, s_oleg, design element

Note to Parents, Teachers, and Librarians
Step-by-Step Stories is a nonfiction set that teaches sequencing skills along with solid information about the
title subjects. Through fun text and photos, this set supports math and science concepts such as order of
events, relative position words, and ordinal positions. Use the exercise on page 28 to help children practice
their sequencing skills.

Printed in the United States of America in North Mankato, Minnesota.
032011   006110CGF11

Table of Contents

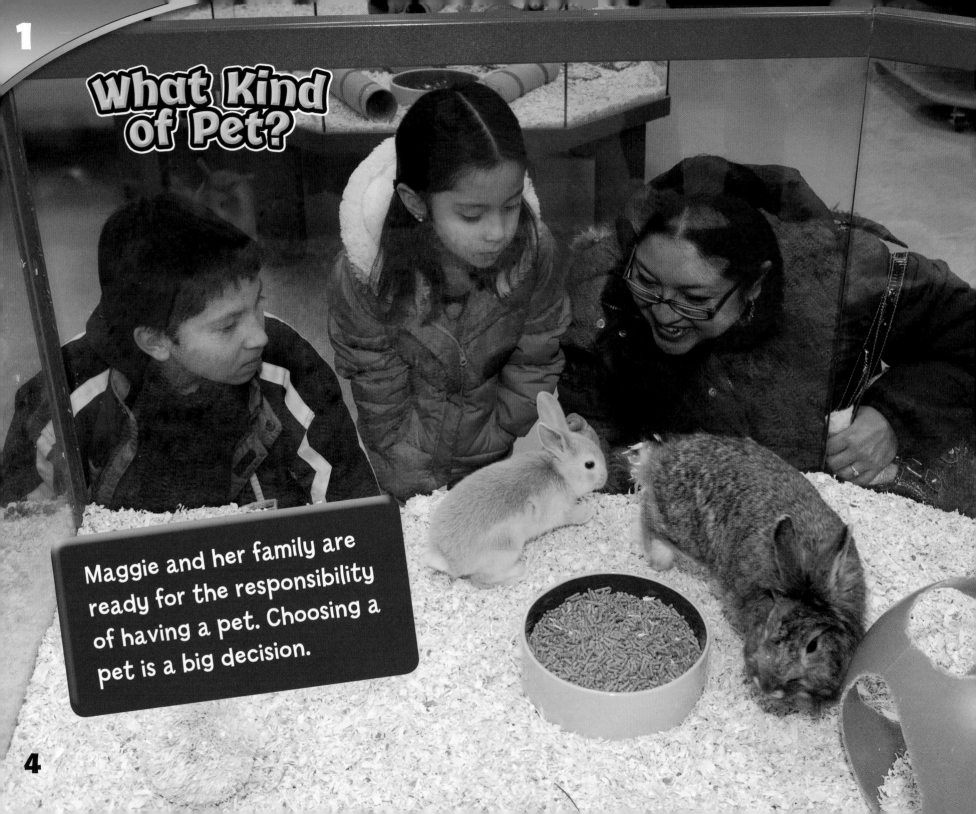

1

What Kind of Pet?

Maggie and her family are ready for the responsibility of having a pet. Choosing a pet is a big decision.

Maggie's family needs to choose a pet that will best suit them. How will they decide which pet to get?

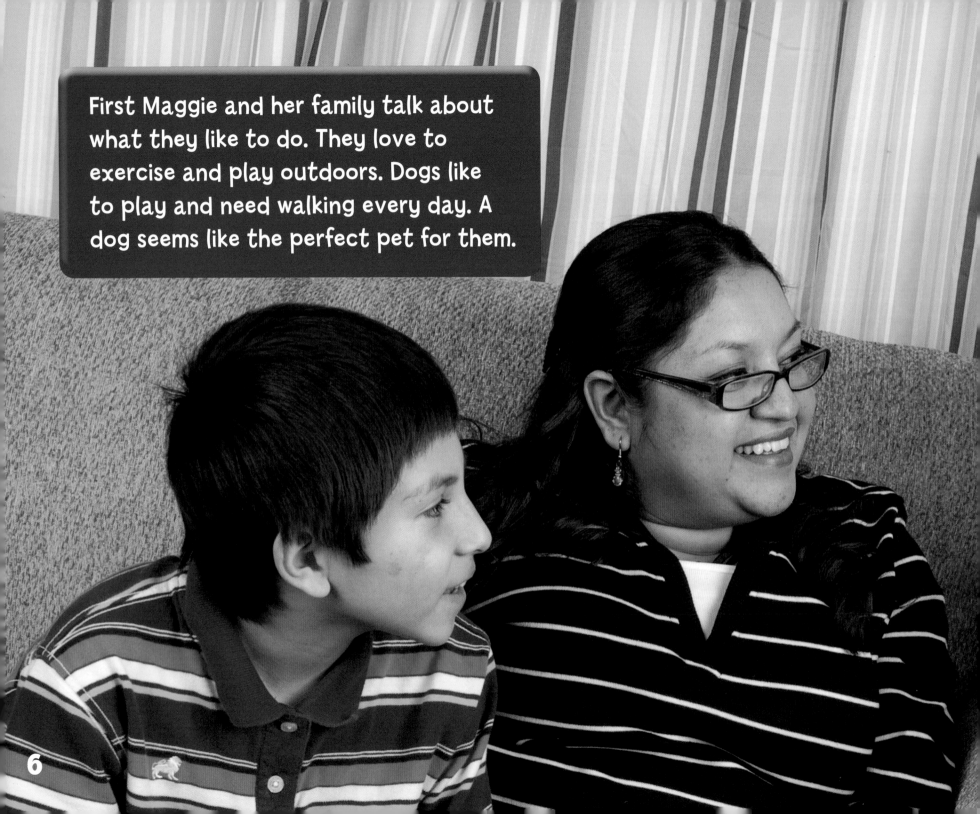

First Maggie and her family talk about what they like to do. They love to exercise and play outdoors. Dogs like to play and need walking every day. A dog seems like the perfect pet for them.

But what about barking? That's not a problem for this noisy family!

Every pet is different. Hamsters play at night. Cats and dogs like to cuddle and play during the day. It's important to find a pet that fits the way you live.

7

2

Narrowing Down the Choices

Maggie's family learns all they can about dogs. They look up dogs on the Internet.

8

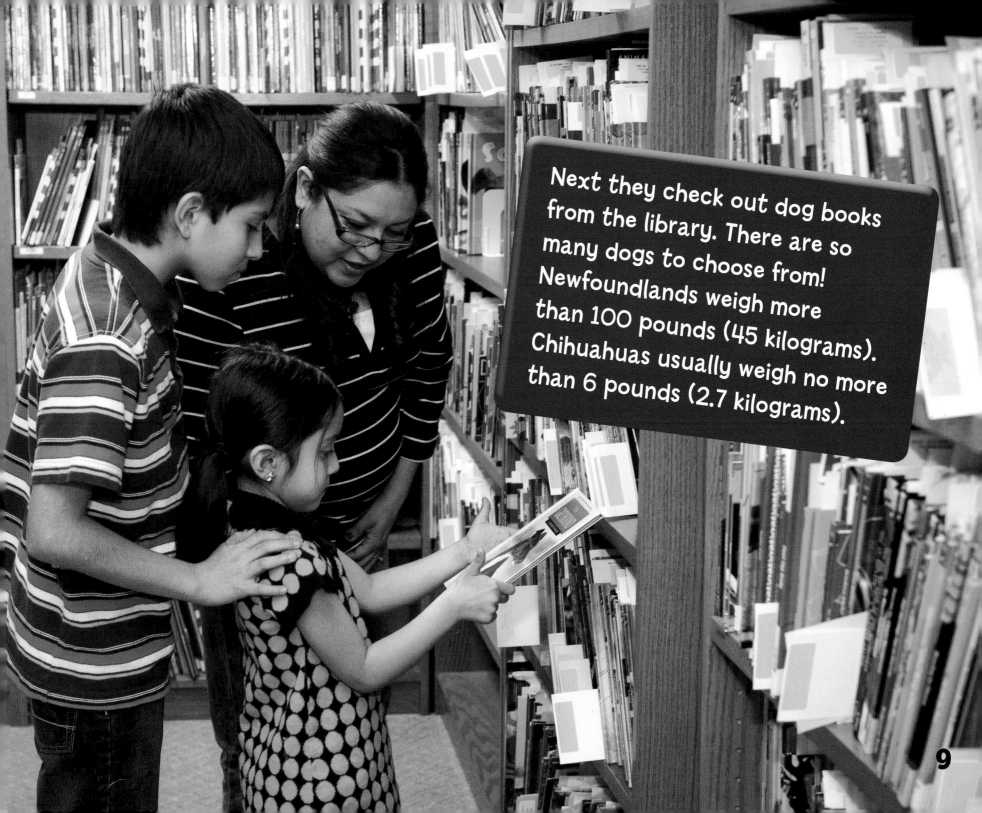

Next they check out dog books from the library. There are so many dogs to choose from! Newfoundlands weigh more than 100 pounds (45 kilograms). Chihuahuas usually weigh no more than 6 pounds (2.7 kilograms).

Maggie's family decides to get a Labrador retriever. Labradors are smart. They are also usually good around kids.

But should Maggie's family get a puppy or an older dog? Puppies take a lot of time to train. Maggie's Mom is busy, so training a puppy would be difficult. They agree to find a dog that's at least 3 years old.

Puppies must be taught basic skills such as greeting people and going to the bathroom outdoors. An older dog may already know these things.

THE GREYHOUND

3

Finding a Pet

Next Maggie's family looks for a dog. They search local newspaper ads and look online. They even visit a pet store. After all the searching, they have no luck!

Then they visit a local breeder. But he has only puppies. What will Maggie's family do?

The breeder gives Maggie's family the address of an animal shelter. Then Maggie and her family visit the shelter.

14

Once there, they look for signs that the animals are well cared for. They make sure the rooms are clean.

Every year millions of animals enter shelters across the United States. Some of these animals stay at the shelters. Others are placed in foster homes.

After checking the shelter, they look closely at the animals. The animals have fresh food and water. They also have plenty of room to play. These are all signs of good care.

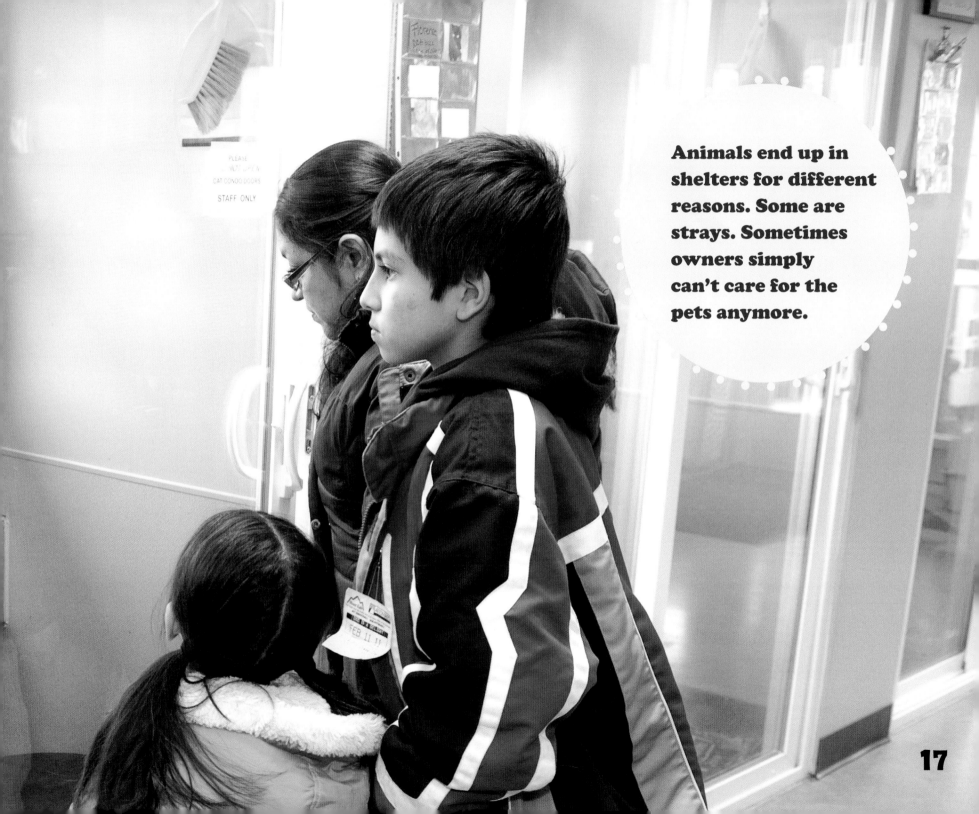

Animals end up in shelters for different reasons. Some are strays. Sometimes owners simply can't care for the pets anymore.

Next Maggie's family meets a woman who cares for the animals. She is really friendly.

She tells them that every pet at the shelter is looked over by a veterinarian. Veterinarians care for injuries and treat illnesses. They also make sure the animals get shots to stay healthy.

19

Maggie tells her what kind of dog they are looking for. The caretaker shows them a dog named Coco.

Dogs aren't the only animals found at pet shelters. Shelters may also have cats, rabbits, birds, and other animals.

To get to know Coco, Maggie and her family take her for a walk. What a great dog! Coco is alert, sits when told, and is housebroken.

4

Preparing for a Pet

Maggie and her family decide to adopt Coco. But before they can take her home, they must get ready for their new pet.

Coco will need a collar and a leash. She will also need bowls for food and water, a brush, and a crate. Toys will make her happy too!

Make sure you give your pet everything it needs. By doing so, you will help your pet live a healthy and happy life.

23

The next day Maggie gets ready to pick up Coco from the shelter.

Maggie puts soft towels inside the crate to help Coco feel safe on her way home. Sometimes frightened pets have accidents. The towels will help keep Coco dry.

Once they get home, Maggie's family lets Coco explore the yard. Then Coco marks their yard as her own by going to the bathroom.

Inside the house, Coco sniffs around to learn everyone's scent. When Coco relaxes, Maggie adds a name tag to the dog's collar. Welcome home, Coco!

27

Mixed-up Mess!

Now that you've learned the steps in getting a pet, can you put these pictures in order?

A Get everything your pet will need.

B Talk about which pet will match your family's interests.

C Learn everything you can about the pet you want to get.

D Welcome your pet home!

Glossary

adopt—to take as one's own

alert—pays attention to people and things

animal shelter—a safe place where lost or homeless pets can stay

breeder—a person who raises animals to sell

crate—a cage

foster home—a safe place where animals can live for a short time

housebroken—trained to go to the bathroom outdoors or in an appropriate place

responsibility—a duty or job

stray—an animal that is lost or without a home

Read More

Davis, Rebecca Fjelland. *Woof and Wag: Bringing Home a Dog.* Get a Pet. Minneapolis: Picture Window Books, 2009.

Driscoll, Laura. *Presidential Pets.* New York: Grossett & Dunlap, 2009.

Feeney, Kathy. *Caring for Your Gerbil.* Positively Pets. Mankato, Minn.: Capstone, 2008.

Internet Sites

FactHound offers a safe, fun way to find Internet sites related to this book. All of the sites on FactHound have been researched by our staff.

Here's all you do:

Visit *www.facthound.com*

Type in this code: 9781429660242

Super-cool stuff! Check out projects, games and lots more at www.capstonekids.com

Index